In Bluebeard's Castle

Miriam Sagan

Many sections first appeared in the blog Miriam's Well
(www.miriamswell.wordpress.com).
"Bread Mystery" was installed at SITE Santa Fe as part of Axle
Project
"Cossack" first appeared in Pyrotechnics
"Elusive", "Fortuna", and "West of the Moon" first appeared in
Boston Poetry Magazine
"Representation" in Eye of Life
"Two Chicks in Hell" in Agnes Project

ISBN 978-1-7326501-3-8

Printed in the United States of America

RED MOUNTAIN PRESS

Santa Fe, New Mexico
www.redmountainpress.us

Part 1

Recklessness

I must have been about thirty when my father informed me of his disappointment and of my failure as a daughter. I was a reckless person, he said, the implication being that I was self-centered and did not care about the damage and concern I had caused to others, i.e. to him, my father. Reckless, reckless, he reiterated in a rage.

My transgressions were threefold, and based on events in my early twenties.
1. I had gotten sick and almost died.
2. My boyfriend had left me.
3. I had not buckled my life jacket promptly on the Colorado River.

This is that story.

I did love my father for many years, maybe quite a lot. When I was a child, he was unattainable, and I wanted him. As a teenager and adult, I both enjoyed him and could finally admit to myself how much I feared him.

The last time he hit me, I was sixteen years old. He wanted the phone, I was on it, and he hauled off and slugged me hard across the face.

This he did not remember and would have denied if confronted. Our relationship remained a touchstone of both good and bad, a riddle I could never solve, a koan I could practice but never truly understand.

When my father was dying, I made two lists—one of things I liked about him, one of things I didn't like. The lists were about the same length. A friend pointed out that that wasn't so bad, considering the men of my father's generation.

Bad Things About My Father

violent
hit me
bully
dominated my mother
thin-skinned
anxious
overly sensitive
made you suffer for crossing him
cheap
unaffectionate
physically uptight
set in his ways
bad-tempered
tantrum thrower
unscientific
pontificator
had kooky ideas
anti-spiritual

Good Things About My Father

handsome
smart
intellectual
sensitive to beauty
loved arts
ambitious
successful
focused
good politics
a real New Yorker
scrappy
can-do
loved my daughter Isabel
loved both my husbands
funny
appreciative
curious
generous

You see my problem.

In Bluebeard's Castle

In the fairy tale, the evil Bluebeard tells his most recent wife she can go into any room in his castle, except for one—a secret locked one. Then he gives her a key to that room. And off he goes. Of course she opens the door. And finds the corpses of his previous wives. Some hanging on hooks. Some moaning as ghosts. And has to be rescued by her sister and brother. It is impossible to go into—and get out of—that room alone.

I've always loved "Life in Hell," a comic strip by Matt Groening, creator of *The Simpsons*. My favorite: one little creature asks another, as they look at the spooky abode on a mountain,"Why do people go into Count Dracula's Castle when it is CALLED Count Dracula's Castle?"

Because we deny the frightening truth about things. Maybe this time the castle will be Club Med. But probably not.

Door Number One

My father and I were having supper at one of Berkeley's innumerable pleasant Chinese restaurants. He was drinking a beer. He wanted to tell me a story.

I was about twenty-eight years old, my father twice that. He was reminiscing about the garment industry, his life before he became a freelance academic. He wanted to tell me something.

"There were two Armenians," he said. "And a safe full of cash. $20,000.00, maybe more. That was worth more then. And these two Armenians…"

He paused. I could tell he was not going to continue. He sipped beer, crumbled some dry wonton into his soup of soft ones.

"So…" he said, changing the subject to the class he was teaching.

He had to stop. This story could only be leading to something between inappropriate and criminal, from bribery to tax evasion to broken kneecaps.

My father paused. In this moment, dimly lit in the red glow of lanterns and pink tablecloths, I would never know who he was.

When he died, more than thirty years later, I would tell this story to my friend Kathleen the novelist, but we would not be able to figure it out. "Armenians can only mean trucking, the trucking business," I said, but that shed no light.

My father liked food that was wrapped in a bland carb: knishes, doughnuts, wonton. There is just a little bit of a surprise, but not too much, when you bite down. After all, the jelly doughnut advertises its jelly, the kasha knish its contents.

I will never know who he is.

Grand Canyon

When I was twenty-four, my fifty-one year old father decided to take me and my fourteen year old brother down the Grand Canyon. The rest of the family did not want to come because they were afraid of snakes. We planned to hike Bright Angel Trail and meet up with a raft trip that would take us down the Colorado River to put out at Lake Powell. To train, I jumped rope—inspired by Mohammed Ali—figuring it worked the down step. I also walked with my backpack full of bricks and books.

We slept at the rim and met up with two others from the trip to hike down. They were doctors, from Chicago. His brother lived in Chicago, my father said.

What neighborhood?

Hyde Park.

Pretty DARK down there, one said.

Not for him, my father retorted.

After their racist remark, my father would barely speak to them as we descended mile after mile, literally dropping in geologic time as visible in layers of rock. I was in ecstasy, but in a way I couldn't quite express. I had never hiked anything—nor would I again—but this was working except for sore calves.

My father hated the Chicago doctors for the rest of the trip. One day we passed a raft on which a woman had split part of her head open in a rapid, on one of the watertight ammo cans used for storage. One of the docs stitched her up, in a dramatic act of kindness to humanity. My father did not soften.

On this trip, there would be many ephemeral meetings that would influence me for the rest of my life. But at first I was mostly focused on not getting sunburned, not falling out of the raft, and figuring out when to pee. Once I found my balance, I observed that the majority of folks on the four rafts were a sprawling interrelated family from L.A.—mostly Jewish. I never quite figured out who was initially married to whom, but I started to get to know them.

There was a guy in his forties, red-headed, who said he was working on a book about how to write screenplays. My father became instantly critical of the Angelenos, while being drawn to them. They were just too...friendly...for his taste. A few years later he'd say, "Remember that guy on the raft trip who claimed to be writing a book? I bet he never did."

"He did," I said.

"But he said it was going to be great. I've never heard of it."

"It's famous," I told him. "The best book of its kind."

"No!"

"Yes. I loved it. It's taught all over the country."

"I thought he was bullshitting," said my father.

All day we floated on the cold, green Colorado, the height of which was controlled by water use in L.A. and the Hoover dam. We floated through time, through rock, striation. Empty granaries left by ancient people watched us from the rim. For the ten days of the trip, we did not see the horizon line. The sun rose, the moon set, the constellations wheeled—and the view was partial. This was the first time in my life that I realized how much I liked to be enclosed, to have my options limited. No way out but through. After this, I sought monk's cells, Zen meditation cushions, motel rooms, trailers out in salt flats, but the canyon was my first container.

We docked each late afternoon to camp and prepare dinner. One of the Angelenos was a sturdy Jewish shrink, a Gestalt type. His teenage son, maybe sixteen, was skinny and fair. I was guessing his mother wasn't Jewish. Every day, the son scrambled up and climbed the canyon wall freehand. He went as high as he could. And his father just stood there, barefoot in the cooling sand, eyes glued to the kid, as if willing his safety. He stood, unable to relax, until the son returned.

Wow, my twenty-four year old self thought. I'm so glad I'll NEVER act like that. Poor father, he should either forbid the kid or ignore him, do something else. Twenty-five years later, when I was the mother of a teenager, that waiting figure would suddenly loom up in my mind's eye, and I'd sympathize.

After dinner, dusk would fall from the increment of sky and then night, a sliver or wedge of its glittering darkness.

The Angelenos had pot, that incredibly strong pot that was starting to be grown in Sonoma and elsewhere. This was not the pot of the 1960's or high school. It had no seeds or stems. It never smelled musty. Its quality was golden and did not vary. One hit got you very very high. This is the pot that people offered with the warning—this stuff is really strong, not what you're used to. Everyone smoked sitting in the cool sand of a tamarisk island, stoned, feeling the dark Colorado rush past us.

"What is that smell?" My father wanted to know one morning. "Every night, it's the same sweet smoke...is it...marijuana...?"

"Probably those guys from Los Angeles," I said.

"Probably," my father agreed.

We did not always agree. A tiny incident would come back to haunt me. One morning, we were sitting in the pontoon raft, putting things in order, waiting to cast off. I was wearing my life jacket, but unbuckled. It was hot, my breasts were a bit too big for it, I could swim, and besides—the raft was firmly tethered to the shore. I expected to buckle it once we entered the river. But my father went ballistic. He ordered me to buckle it. He yelled. He looked terrified. I was furious, but I buckled it. I had no idea what he was so upset about.

The trip had its Hemingwayesqe themes, too—sexy guides and fascinated tourists. The leader was a very handsome bad boy type. He was soon obviously embroiled in a hot two week stand with a pretty, slightly older than him, chic Angeleno. When we came to the end of the trip, at take out, the leader's live-in girlfriend was waiting, ecstatic to see him. An earth madonna in granny dress and long curly hair, she threw her arms around him. Tensions rippled into good-byes.

Wow, I thought. I'm glad that isn't me. However, it soon would be.

We all said good-bye, and my father and brother went back to New Jersey. I went to Flagstaff and caught a train that was many hours late and went to San Francisco. I was spending part of the summer with a former college roommate on upper Polk Street, although I was ostensibly living with my boyfriend in Boston. At the end of the summer, when I returned, this boyfriend would break up with me, throwing me into a depressive tail spin that would last for two years.

My relationship with my father was forever complicated by his accusations of my recklessness. Perhaps he was saying these things, including the unbuckled life jacket, had frightened him? Perhaps he felt he was also watching me climb freehand to the rim? I did not ask.

The canyon stayed with me, though, and the river. No doubt forever. A few years later my brother and I were looking at a large scale model of the Grand Canyon in the Boston Museum of Science. Look—we were there. Look—that's the falls. With a sense of ownership, we stepped over the rope barring the public and started touching points on the model.

A security guard appeared and hauled us off.

Incognito

When we were children, my father was not very available. He came home after dinner, worked late on Thursdays, and a half day Saturday. He and my mother went out Saturday night until he put a stop to that by abruptly refusing to socialize ever again. No parties, no dinners, no couples. He announced this at age forty, and pretty much held to it for the next forty-eight years.

When he was home, my father often said he was "incognito." I thought it was an actual place, called Cognito. Perhaps it was, as it meant he was in his study with the door closed. If he emerged briefly, he refused to answer if spoken to. He was not to be disturbed, and never was.

From this remove, I have the urge to diagnose. Sensitivity? Hypoglycemia? Asperger's? Whatever it was, my father believed that his preferences and reactions were right, the morally correct course. A hatred of small talk was not just his quirk, or a personal preference. It was an elevated position, one that any superior person would automatically take. I, who even now enjoy a chat about the weather, fruit trees, real estate, gossip, and clothes, had to rally my childish resources to discuss the ancient Greeks.

Surprisingly, my father had four children. That was a lot of people to fend off. He eventually had five sons and daughters-in-law, and seven grandchildren. And he did not really want any of us under his roof.

Once, after an extraordinarily rare visit with a friend, he complained about the vagaries of being a houseguest. His hosts were so picky about the kitchen, the sponges, the faucets.

"Yes," I agreed. "And it's not just hard to be a good houseguest but to be a good host."

"True," my father said. "And you know, I've had a lot of houseguests."

"You have?" I was surprised. I could literally not come up with an instance when a visitor not of my own generation had slept under my father's roof.

"Of course...you, your sisters, your brother..."

So after our lives together my father regarded his children as guests. No wonder he most often tried to dissuade us from visiting, citing the domestic upheaval of having to change the sheets. Once, in my fifties, I offered to bring a sleeping bag, but he didn't laugh.

West of the Moon

outside
the motel window
desert spring afternoon

two mourning doves
nesting on the top
of a parking lot lamp

I'm waiting
for it to rain
beyond the sliding screen

I'm waiting
for my childhood
to run off

on its bare
skinny legs
and grass-stained knees

dusk, and they've flown
off, a dry wind
in this drought

propped
against the white pillows
my memories remain.

Fortuna

my eyes full of salt
where is the mirror that remembers?
there is no ointment
to salve time

once you loved me
I'm sure of it
you love me still
I'm sure of that also

if the stars chart a course
or you chart a course by the stars
open your hand
no palm reader knows Braille

what I saw but didn't understand
what I didn't see
and everything hidden
that no dove or raven found in me.

Psyche in Darkness

a stolen child
a half dozen
bulbs
of pink lilies

sunlight
in the leaves
even this flutter
can't bring back the lost

a file
of missing persons
the blind mole
the earthworm

sunflowers
raise their faces
to the race
of time

as do you
pregnant virgin
bleeding grandmother
everything

that gives birth
to its opposite.

In The House of Israel

I'll tell this story. It is the first thing on my father's list that he held against me.

Why? I am in my sixties, crippled on my right side, with half a lung. I am scarred over twenty-five percent of my torso. I've been in chronic pain for over forty years. Essentially I am disabled, a state I have ignored, treated, hidden, and expressed. Although each approach has seemed exciting and important at the time, something is always lacking.

A narrative.

How? Decade after decade, I will avoid this topic. Then suddenly I will find myself in the interior of Bluebeard's castle, opening the frightening locked doors of my story. I am not propelled towards this by a therapeutic breakthrough, a traumatic event, or an act of personal redemption. Simply, my father has a stroke, and dies, and can't read what I write anymore.

However, I cannot write this alone. My friend Kathleen and I have set up a series of writing dates—at her house, the library, a cafe. We both write our own material, and then read to each other.

Her presence makes this possible.

Where? I have actually entered another gigantic ominous building, a place of death and dismemberment and perhaps survival. It is not Bluebeard's fairy tale castle, but the Beth Israel Hospital in Boston.

It began when my boyfriend got strep throat. Of course I continued to make out with him. He was a handsome WASP, tall, dark-haired. and too cute for me really with his high cheekbones and athletic build. He was a total runaround. If I neglected him for fifteen minutes or left a dull party early, he'd run off with some other woman. So I kissed him despite his white-spotted tonsils.

Soon, I was sick with a fever. I was a year ahead of most of my friends in college, and had graduated the previous spring. I lived on Mass. Ave. in a cavernous apartment with an old friend. My boyfriend was still in the dorms, working on his thesis about the Swedish penal system, an admiring view for its efficacy and lack of recidivism.

I went to a clinic in north Cambridge and tested negative for strep. I did not have health insurance, wasn't even really aware of the need for it, a fact overlooked by my family. I was teaching part-time and trying to become a writer. I had been rejected from grad school, and was reapplying. I lived on a tight budget and ate mostly bagels, doughnuts, and coffee. I did not have a doctor in Boston.

My fever got worse. It spiked 104 and I went to Cambridge City Hospital in the middle of the night. I had an agonizing pain on the right side. In that crowded hell of an ER I was not given a chest X-ray, was prescribed Valium and sent home.

Over the next few days I grew steadily worse, sleeping a lot and reading the depressing, if proto-feminist, diaries of Sophia Tolstoy, and having worried disoriented love-making sessions to keep my boyfriend faithful.

My parents were in New Jersey, but my father taught once a week in Boston. They did not invite me to come home, nor did I ask. I'd been sick with an intestinal infection over the winter holidays, and the family physician had said: you're not as sick as you think you are. My mother concurred. I was a bother, she'd have to do more driving, shopping, etc.

My parents were vaguely aware that I was sick in Boston. Call Dr. Z., my father suggested. He was a doctor I had seen once for something minor in the autumn. I called, and he berated me forcefully: I've told you before there is nothing wrong with you! Stop calling this office. I won't speak to you again.

Horrified, I hung up the phone.

I later found out that he had confused me with another patient. He actually tracked me down months later when I was hospitalized to apologize, and to say he hoped he hadn't been part of my inability to get care. Although of course he had been.

I went again to Cambridge City Hospital, was again sent home with a diagnosis of flu. I then, half unconsciously, must have settled in to either live or, more likely, die. A clinic, two ER visits, a doctor, my parents, and my friends did not think there was anything seriously wrong with me. I must have been making it up, I concluded, or "overreacting" as I was often accused of doing. The excruciating pain on my right side, which I later found out was called devil's grip pleurisy, and the high fever were messages I was now set to ignore.

My father, however, was concerned enough to stop by on his way to the weekly class he taught in Boston. He took one look at me, called a cab, and took me to the Beth Israel Hospital, which in those days was an enormous chaotic center looming over the slums of the Fenway and Roxbury beyond. I was wearing jeans and a loose white Indian tunic embroidered in purple. No bra—it was too painful. Also, a tiny ring of yellow enamel flowers, which was a token from my boyfriend. I had my purse, but otherwise not so much as a toothbrush.

I was admitted from the ER and given a room. They wanted a sputum sample, but my lungs no longer had the strength to expel anything. I was given a lung tap with a local anesthetic block on the skin of my back. The pain was so severe that I screamed uncontrollably, completely disoriented, unaware that the sounds were emanating from me. "Would someone please tell that woman screaming down the hall to shut up," I murmured.

Dr. Frank, a famous surgeon, decided to cut me open. My parents were no doubt distraught, but also on reassuring turf, a Jewish hospital, a famous surgeon. In fact, in this very same Jewish hospital my paternal grandfather had been given one of the first pacemakers to ever be installed and my maternal grandfather had been diagnosed and treated for tuberculosis of the liver. This was the B.I. This was Boston, covered in sleet and snow and rain, but the greatest medical center on my family's map. Indeed, its name was House of Israel.

Elusive

the column has a woman's face
a serene expression that can bear weight

weedy and overgrown in summer's deep
day embroidered with tiger lilies

a mystical temple, disused, abandoned
on a hill overlooking the housing development

a line of straight pins stuck in a tablecloth
she alters the silken kimono

from picture postcard souvenir
or a draped robe or shroud.

one caryatid balances darkness
one wears the horns of light

fate snaps with her scissors,
day, night

Resurrection

Dr. Frank performed surgery along the lines of a thoracotomy, cut on my right side, although he did not remove my ribs. Two tubes were inserted to drain the lung. Pleurisy had become empyema, a stew of anaerobic organisms in the right lung, a famous killer in the nineteenth century but almost unknown after the discovery of antibiotics. The left lung had collapsed from stress. There was pneumonia in both. An I.V. fed a broad-spectrum antibiotic into my veins, along with frequent doses of morphine. A mask delivered oxygen and a warm mist. The draining machine bubbled.

The doctors informed my parents that I would most probably die.

I lay in the I.C.U., dying. Several visions tipped me off to my critical state. The first was that my soul left my body and my point of view changed. I saw everything as if from above, the I.C.U., the blinking green lights and hiss of the machinery, my body in the bed. This was disconcerting for many reasons, not the least of which was that I had not been raised to believe in the existence of the soul. But something was certainly no longer in my body.

I also approached a thick black line somewhere in an alternate reality, came up against it as if it were an actual wall, and quite purposively decided not to cross it. And finally, I saw huge gates open and rays of light stream out.

I had been raised as an atheist. My father worshipped Marx and Freud. This was before the popularization of Kubler-Ross's writing, or the use of the phrase "near death experience." I simply assumed that those majestic light filled gates were the towers of the George Washington Bridge that had somehow been transposed to the I.C.U. Afterwards, for many years, I spoke of these experiences to no one.

Six weeks passed in the I.C.U. Soon, I was a victim of sleep deprivation psychosis. I was awakened every four hours, and my vitals were checked. I experienced complete dissociation from my body and surroundings. I begged the staff: "Please put the body of the girl back into the bed. I know that only moments ago there was the body of a young girl in the bed."

I meant myself, of course, but had lost the orientation to say so. I also couldn't recall my name. But I knew that wasn't good. So I'd sneak peeks at my wrist, where my name was clearly printed on a hospital bracelet: MIRIAM SAGAN. It did look familiar.

A young intern took pity on me.

"You have sleep deprivation psychosis," he said as I sobbed that I didn't know where I was. "You're in the B.I." he told me.

"Of course!" It all came back to me.

"And you're doing better than most people with it," he added. "Usually I can never convince them they're here."

I felt better. My condition had a name. I was doing better than most people (music to a student's ears.). But I was still insane.

"Then let me sleep," I pleaded. "Hey," I continued, struck by a clever if paranoid notion. "I bet you twenty-five cents you won't let me sleep."

I thought I could motivate him for the sum of a quarter. He did let me sleep, and I am still grateful after all these years. And they stopped waking me for the vitals. I could remember my name again, and that I was the body in the bed.

Things went less smoothly with another young guy, the psychiatric intern.

"How does it feel to be twenty-one and have almost died?" he asked me, pen and pad poised.

"Get out!" I screamed. I was sitting half naked on the bedside commode. And I wasn't about to talk to an insensitive nerdy guy my own age. Besides, I had no idea how to answer the question.

Eventually, I was transferred up to the post-operative ward, a world of its own. In contrast to the I.C.U. it was dynamic and dramatic, full of people and action. At this Jewish hospital, visiting hours were not enforced. A gypsy patriarch was next door, attended by about forty people who slept in the room and corridor. The women had voluminous petticoats and scarves. A small boy, the only English speaker, translated for the doctors.

The gypsies ate delicious smelling sandwiches. An army of the post-operative, some missing limbs, patrolled the corridors on mandatory walks. People screamed in pain, laughed, made loud phone calls. Children ran up and down. Only late at night did things quiet down. A kindly Jamaican aide would come in to mop and would help me turn over in bed, an agonizing procedure.

Soon, I could walk the ward and beyond, pushing my I.V. My mother asked if I had a robe. I said I had a blue and white striped one, hospital issue. When she visited, she was appalled by the thing. It was ratty and washed out. "You made it sound nice," she said accusingly. One more thing was my fault—I was badly dressed. She bought me two caftans that swam on my starved body. I had lost my entire adult weight and stopped menstruating. My hair was braided. When my roommate visited she burst into tears. I looked just as I had when we were in the sixth grade. Every morning a cheery, slightly plump nurse would weigh me. Often, I'd have lost another half pound. I'd weep, to her jealous consternation. I was still on a liquid diet.

One lunch, my tray appeared with a serving of Swedish meatballs. I wolfed them down, my first solid food in months. Then, overcome by a worried intuition, I checked the order slip. It was for a Mrs. Finklestein. I'd eaten her meatballs. But as there was no ill effect, I was allowed solid food.

My chest was in agony. I had a railroad track scar over twenty-five percent of my body. A half of my right lung was destroyed. I would be in chronic pain for the rest of my life. No one discussed any of this with me.

I was also abruptly detoxed from weeks on morphine. "Now that you are going to live," yet another intern told me, "I don't want to send you out in the street addicted to something you know the name of." He put me on extra strength Bufferin, which surprisingly worked quite well. However, he was right. I have always promised myself that I'd experience morphine again before I die. It made an impression.

After that, things progressed quickly. Visitors no longer had to suit up in masks and discardable paper outfits. I came off the heavy I.V., my arm battered and bruised but set free. The hospital asked me to meet with another young woman who had also had her lungs collapse with the flu. They asked us to track our whereabouts before we got sick—bars, parties, friends. She'd gone to Boston College. We had been nowhere in common. This was before the widespread use of computers, but we had tripped some epidemiological line.

What had happened to me? Forty years later, when swine flu was in the news, I had two medical professionals tell me that it looked like I'd had swine flu.

Well, I told myself towards the end of my hospital stay, I don't want to do THAT again. Die, that is. Well, I amended it, I don't ever want to do that again as an AMATEUR.

I meant, as an innocent, an idiot, a person who did not know life. I wasn't even twenty-two years old, and my old life was over. Indeed, the former me had died. I was, mostly unwittingly, in the first moments of becoming someone else.

The last night in the B.I. I attempted to pour myself a glass of water and dropped the pitcher with my weakened and crippled right arm. I soaked the hospital bed. No one answered the call button. I stripped off the sheets and slept under my winter coat on a bare mattress in one of the greatest hospitals in the world.

The next day I was discharged. I had been released into my parents' care. I had fought the doctors on this, but they had insisted it was either a nursing home or New Jersey. I couldn't fly home because of my lungs. My father said he'd drive me. I put on the purple embroidered shirt and my own underwear. The little ring of enamel flowers, though, was sadly lost forever.

That first night out we stayed at the Copley Plaza, where my parents had been married, to rest up for the drive. I had my own room. My dad let me invite my boyfriend for room service dinner. We shared an avocado stuffed with crabmeat and each ate a steak. I caught a glimpse of us making love in a mirrored wardrobe and I looked terrifying, like a barely developed teenager. A violent red scar with railroad track cross hatchings burned across my torso.

A few hours before, I'd been anxious, getting out of the cab and having to cross the lobby of the hotel.

"What will people think when they see me?" I asked my father. I was also afraid someone would bump into my painful right side.

"Don't worry," he said. "No one will know what has happened to you. You just look like you've had a mental breakdown."

At the time, distressed as I was, I found this re-assuring. Although now that my father is dead, decades later, I like his response less. Why was a mental break-down somehow more acceptable than almost dying? Was it something he expected of me—mental collapse? It was the start of my parents' total refusal to ever discuss my illness and surgery. And yet at that moment I just wished that he would also say he was sorry about what had hap-pened to me.

However, it is obvious now that my father did indeed save my life. And that I never thanked him. I'm not sure he felt thanks were due—he was my father after all, and in his own way committed to that role.

A few years ago, I had the startling realization that alt-hough my experience in the B.I. was of being traumatized and tortured, that was not the doctors' and nurses' intent at all. I understood quite vividly, and for the first time, that to them I was a desperately ill young person—someone's child—who they would try and save. As a result, I wrote the B.I. an anonymous letter thanking them. I enclosed $36.00 in cash. In Jewish mysticism, the number 18 stands for chai, or life. Charity is often given in "double chai" or amounts of thirty-six. It is spiritually efficacious for both giver and receiver.

And the time has also come for me to say the same thing to my father. Thank you.

Rhina

It was not easy for many of my generation to survive the kind of families we were born into, even if they were middle or upper middle class. Or perhaps it would be more accurate to say it was not easy to survive the transition from child to adult in the 1960's in a family like mine. A case in point was Rhina, the eldest daughter of my father's best friend. I always liked Rhina, loved her even, and was thrown in with her in the vague way that children are friends with the children of their parent's friends. Her father was a film director, who gained serious renown. My father was in the garment business. They both had four children, in the same constellation, three girls and a boy.

Rhina was a gentle moon-faced child, pretty and sweet. Her family was considered to be poor by mine, and also by her own parents, before her father hit the big time. This poverty was expressed during one visit to their house where we were all expected to share one bathtub of water. Rhina's father proposed a system: he'd draw the bath and the two youngest would bathe as a pair, and on up. One tub of water for eight children. I squirmed. There was sociable bathing among my sibs, but I was hyper aware of how often the little ones liked to pee in the tub.

My father must have sensed something because he countered that Rhina and I should get the first bath, which we did.

My memories of her are scattered but always pleasant: playing in a fort of lawn furniture, a California Christmas without snow, watching her dance in a local production of the *Nutcracker*. And more economy—a holiday tree decorated with paper snowflakes and popcorn chains.

The last time I saw her was when we were teenagers. She was California hip, but still very gentle. I felt no criticism from her petite feminine self. Besides, by then I was secure in my own emerging hipness, New York tough and not a virgin.

I remember she took me and my sister to a warren of headshops and cafes in an L.A. neighborhood, a little shopping for love beads and peace signs, coffee, and sitting on the ground against a warm wall in that lovely California sun.

Then she killed herself. We were both eighteen, late winter, second semester Freshman year. I'd come home for spring break and ended up in bed with mono. The news came. Rhina had committed suicide.

There were bad boyfriends or helpless ones. There was heroin, and pills for migraines. Her family had gone to Europe for a year of her father's shoot. Over Christmas, she locked herself in the bathroom of the house and took an overdose.

Rescued, she was sent back to college. Her psychiatrist reassured her parents she was not seriously suicidal. She had an A average. She left an affectionate note of apology and OD'd in her parents' bed.

It was not easy to survive. My own mother blamed the Sixties and Hollywood. Three years later, doctors at the Beth Israel hospital told my parents I was dying and they did not think they could save me. Rhina was waving, now permanently younger than me in life and older than me as a ghost.

Almost thirty years later, I was able to do something for Rhina, or in her memory, or for the sweet girl who still resided with me, although pale, faded, and transparent. My own daughter had had her heart broken, and wanted to drop out of college and come home. All my training, my family ethos, was to tell her to buck up, stick it out. Instead, I just told her: come home. Now. We're paying for the airplane ticket. Come.

When I got off the phone I said out loud: Rhina, this is for you. Someone's life is going to be saved. Someone gets to go home. It wasn't me or you, but it is someone. This is for you.

Two Chicks in Hell

It's noisy——like a bar
City street, distant siren
Crowded and hot

I've come this way
Trying to get back
My boyfriend—Aphrodite sent me

To see you, Queen of the Dead,
Persephone, the raped, the took
La Chingada, as they say

In Spanish. Look,
I've figured some things out
Some not

Fire ants have kindly left the nest
To help me sort
A heap of beans, a sieve of grains

And long grass, green reeds
Told me not to
Destroy myself

And a tower
Told me about a cave
A less traveled detour.

I'll sit on the ground
Won't eat much of anything
Won't snort a line or bolt a shot

Or lick the rim for salt.
You call me Psyche, that's my name,
Offer me

A mirror and a compact.
Something to powder my nose
Smear my lips

It's beauty, or it's sleep's refrain
As they say, let's not
Go down the alley of the fucked again.

You have to stay,
You married in,
I get to go

Back up to sunlight,
I'm pregnant, can't you see
I'll keep this baby

Cupid's kid
Tattoo upon this broken heart
Its lid.

Reckless

My father accused me of being reckless, but he had no real idea of how reckless I really was in my twenties. My father's specifics didn't hold water, but his worry was based on something more ephemeral, a feeling, a vibe. In this, he was correct.

After I got out of the Beth Israel Hospital I was convinced for many months that I was dead. I felt disembodied, surprised people could see me. My boyfriend and I went to a reggae concert. I was wearing, uncharacteristically, a backless top. I felt too vulnerable, my scar running jaggedly across my back. I kept expecting other dancers to step on me as if I wasn't there.

One of my father's accusations was that my boyfriend had broken up with me. This was true, but I hadn't been able to do anything about it. I was devastated. I was now twenty-four years old, and had just dropped out of graduate school to see if I could become a writer. My heart was broken as well as my body. I lay on the floor day after day in a complete state of despair. I had lost everything except my cat, a scrawny aloof creature who nonetheless provided comfort. I decided I would kill myself. However, I was reading the *Alexandria Quartet*. *Justine* was so beautifully written, I continued. In the subsequent books, events were told from different points of views, plots twisted, secrets were revealed. I kept reading. Hundreds of pages later I had recovered just enough to not commit suicide.

But I was not truly well. I spent a fruitless year and a half in that apartment, leaving as often as I could to go to writers' colonies where I wrote a little, flirted a lot, and moped in scenic surroundings. I had inherited some money from my grandfather, and could live modestly without working. That was perhaps unfortunate, as work would have given me some structure. I tried therapy and went to someone in my father's social network. I had a session with a fascinating older woman who seemed to get me. She immediately developed lung cancer and referred me to another Boston psychoanalyst. He was physically enormous, and mostly silent in sessions. When he spoke, he made a racist remark. I couldn't stand him, but I couldn't quite leave him. I wept and worried in his presence without feeling helped until that too petered out.

I was essentially at the end of my resources when I moved to San Francisco. There, I had acquired two love interests. It was a lot more than anything I had in Boston. Both of my sweeties were Libras, a sign which is said to like balance. I soon added a third Libra. Quickly, all the Libras were enraged with me—I was flakey, unable to commit, likely to sleep with their friends and roommates, unemployed, weepy, and generally an unfaithful downer.

I just couldn't love, I told myself.

Instead I rode on the back of motorcycles. I also spent hours curled in a ball on my futon in my room in one or another communal house. I worried those around me, but they were relative strangers and didn't have much stake in me. I had come to the edge of the continent and things had not improved. I went north to some remote women's land to work on a magazine about woman's spirituality, past Mount Shasta, near Wolf Creek. I made friends among the editors and typesetters, including a woman named Ruby. We smoked against the rules and snuck out to eat bacon and drink coffee at a diner where I'd also washed my hair in the sink of the women's room. Women's land lacked meat, caffeine, and hot water.

Ruby and I were leaving at the same time and decided to hitchhike. A guy in a big rig picked us up. First, he showed us his gun. Then he told us about "two Eskimo princesses" he'd picked up and had sex with at the same time.

On a break by the side of the road Ruby and I looked at each other. "Is he going to rape us?" I asked her.

"I don't think so," she said. A few hours later, safely in the city, I told myself: well, Mir, this is the end of your hitchhiking.

It was the end of more than that. It was a turning point, one that was not obvious at the time. I knew I had done something extremely reckless, getting back into the truck. That was what haunted me. Sure, nothing happened and I trusted Ruby, but she was just guessing. I didn't want to keep getting back into the truck.

I went into therapy in San Francisco. After the first session the therapist said: "I'll work with you but only if you agree not to kill yourself or arrange to be off-ed in the next week."

How did she know? Death was written all over me, but no one else could read it. She was a wise person who helped me enormously. But even then I couldn't explain what I didn't really know—my feeling that since I was already dead, having died in the B.I., it didn't matter if I lived.

But live I did. A few years later I was in my family's beach house when the phone rang late at night.

The operator said: will you accept a collect call from Thanatos?

No, I shouted, and slammed the phone down.

The phone rang again. It was just my brother, thinking he was funny.

But I no longer wanted to accept a collect call from death.

When I Was Young,
I Put Myself in Harm's Way

hoping to get hurt
or at least
fall off the back of a motorcycle
and break my heart

how, now past sixty, I'll still
go out of my way
and travel some cardinal direction or other
saying, I just want to see
(volcano, glacier, Miami Beach)

before it is too late
for me, or it,
and put myself in the way of beauty
and let her have her way with me.

Part 2

Garment Industry

My father's office was composed of a showroom, his large formal office, a warren of small offices behind glass that housed adding machines and payroll, and the cutting room, which was like a small factory. It was a warehouse space, partitioned off, and we took a freight elevator up, creaking and shaking. There were front elevators too, gilt and mirrored, direct to the showroom, for the buyers. There were two worlds—the rough masculine industrial world of production and the well-lit feminine world of beauty and retail. Coats. Coats paid for our white pillared house in the suburbs. Our braces. Our yearly bicycles. My collection of tiny fabric mice dressed as Victorian ladies or Tudor queens in bits of lace and ribbon. Big coats paid for tiny ones. I always had coats. Lots and lots of them.

Coats began their lives as samples, created on the giant tables beneath the flourescent lights of the cutting room. Cutters were the star athletes of the trade—rapid, precise, macho. Each part of the coat, looking anatomical, was drawn on paper and cut to create the pattern. The cutters then used the parts to trace the shape on cloth. They marked with fat pieces of soft chalk, like bars of soap, white and red. They outlined, then cut. They wielded a small deadly saw, giant bladed scissors. It was noisy. Dust and threads flew from the fabric. They coughed. The older cutters were Jewish, the younger, fastest ones were often Puerto Rican. They seemed to work at breakneck speed, as if this were an emergency. More coats! Now! After a sample was cut, it was sewn right there on a machine. A sample represented hundreds or thousands of coats, all its near clones. A sample was shown to the buyer, who was the most important person in the chain. A buyer, say from Sears or Penney's, would choose a sample and then order "the lot" made in its image.

This was when cash changed hands. A buyer expected to be bribed, a cash kickback, perhaps a percentage of the whole. Some buyers were noted, at least in my father's mind, for being honest, an unusual stance but one that he praised. And now that I write this, I realize, of course, benefitted from.

A few buyers were women, tough, tough broads, usually Irish or Jewish, pioneers into a cutthroat retail world. Buyers also lavished us with gifts—cases of whiskey no one in my family drank for Christmas, holiday baskets of fruit and nuts, showy floral arrangements for the birth of a baby.

My father exuded admiration for both cutters and buyers—those who needed to please him and those he needed to please. He'd claim to hate the business and yet he gave it loving attention, and shared his love of it with me. How else could I, a child of eight or nine, know the skill of cutters and the corruption but good taste of buyers?

Of course, the kickbacks were illegal, cash based, and an evasion of federal and state taxes. This was one of the weak links that would later call down a crusading district attorney and a grand jury investigation of the entire industry. But I did not understand that until much later, and I'm guessing that in some way my father did not either. Did he expect to get caught by the laws of the land? I'm guessing no. My grandfather George, a product of tsarist Russia, certainly regarded his own illegal activities as a matter of course—without much guilt or fear. My father, who identified with the second generation of gangsters in *The Godfather*, may have been softer, more Americanized. But I don't think fear of getting caught kept him up at night. I imagine he considered it a possibility, but dismissed it.

The coats were beautiful. The showroom was lined in enormous portable garment racks, stacked lengthwise, making a forest of coats. I'd climb among them, balancing on the lower metal bars so they wouldn't start sliding on their little wheels.

I found the perfect winter coat. It was white, perhaps just a touch towards ivory. It had a dark red velveteen collar, so soft, so plush. A line of buttons covered in the same velvet. Ditto a bit of piping. It fit perfectly. Tight in the waist. Two faux pockets, not for putting things in, just for the line.

I wanted that coat, a not unrealistic expectation, as we often just took samples off the rack. But my mother said no. White would get dirty. She had the shop make it up in a dark blue, looser at the waist, at least with the red trim. One for me, and one for each of my sisters. They were nice coats too, but not the one I yearned for. It was wasted practicality on my mother's part, that durable blue. We never wore a coat for more than a few months. I had at least a new fall coat, a new winter, and a new spring coat each calendar year.

I wanted the white coat with the red velvet collar. The Queen would prick her finger and drops would fall on snow, red blood, in a forest of leafless birches. A firebird would swoop out of the sky. Prince Ivan would shoot a swan who was really a girl.

I'd wanted that coat.

As a child
at City Ballet
I never understood
why the prince wanted
the dorky princess in her nightie
when he could go out with
FIREBIRD
in her red tutu.

I don't think I realized
she was a bird.
(Actually
it was Maria Tallchief
dancing).

Cossack

The archer prince with his Turkish bow
And his Mongol hat aims an arrow

The white-breasted sun shot at solstice
Tumbles from the sky in a corona of feathers

Don't say I never loved you
Or failed to feed you dumplings

"Death to the Jews"
Spray painted on the uneven brick wall

"Russia for the Russians"
"Death to the Muslims"

Babushka holds a child
Overhead the roar of warplanes

Inside, crumbs of black bread
And a mouse called starvation

I'll never be at peace with the unrolled
Double helix of my chromosomes

Or how one matreshka doll
Fits inside another, and another, and so on.

Bread Mystery

in the uncountable alphabet
bitter pine forest of words
sans serif
without butter or jam

one day we'll eat earth
and cry for more!
drink tea through a sugar cube
in italics

how is the strand of wheat
bent heavy with seed
supposed to speak
without being ground?

the night was aphasic
and the day
also said nothing
had nothing to say

it's winter, and the wild
girl goddess has gone under—
"why me" is not a question
that bears repeating

this dough will rise
in the starter of spring
and its crust can be opened
by the mouse teeth of desire

white bread like the moon
in the eastern sky
full, sliced, gone—
round again.

Ancestors

My grandfather, George Sagan, founded the New York Girl Coat Company in 1916. That was not his real name. He was born Gershon Liesenbaum in the Ukraine, a borderland between the Austro-Hungarian Empire and the Holy Russian one, between Kiev and Odessa.

Gershon became George in America. But until the late twentieth century we did not know that our family name was not Sagan. My father had found George's exit visa from Russia. It was for Liesenbaum.

My father searched for an answer in his own imagination. George had bought Mr. Liesenbaum's exit visa. Or, George had murdered Mr. Liesenbaum for the visa. My father actually proposed this theory without irony. My grandfather's power to impose his will was legendary, and survived even his physical death.

The most likely answer was more mundane. My grandfather Gershon, a young teenager, was in the Ukraine with his sister and her three children. She died. He was entrusted with bringing his two little nephews and one niece to their father Louie in New York City. Louie may have already re-married at this point. It is likely that Louie's last name was Sagan.

George tied nephews and niece together with a rope so he wouldn't lose them on shipboard. At Ellis Island, it probably made sense to take their and his brother-in-law Louie's last name, Sagan.

One of the children tied to the rope grew up. He attempted to get an education but by the Great Depression found himself working in the garment industry for George, as one of the prime cutters. His son was Carl Sagan, the famous astronomer. On his deathbed, Carl told one of my first cousins who was interested in family history: "You aren't really a Sagan. The Sagans were the smart side of the family." George's descendants were educated and successful. But we'd been told, and had to believe, we weren't smart like the Sagans, i.e. Carl. And in fact we weren't Sagans, but Liesenbaums.

In his own way, my grandfather cared not just about material success but beauty and justice. However, it was the justice of a gangster and the beauty of a robber baron that drove him.

The iconic story told about him was George's meeting with the famous if perhaps second string Jewish gangster Lepkey. When my grandfather opened for business it was in a storefront on the lower east side. One of Lepkey's henchmen came around and dunned George for protection money, the price of doing business, to be paid every Wednesday. Of course he paid.

A few months later, a second henchman appeared, demanding protection money to be paid on Fridays. My grandfather rebelled. He, a callow youth, demanded a meeting with Lepkey. He was taken to a dairy restaurant on Avenue B., a table in back, men in hats.

George made his speech about justice—he would pay once, but not twice.

Lepkey nodded in his fedora. Then, he offered my grandfather a job, working for him. George politely declined, paid protection but once a week, and went on to make millions.

This story was told in my family not so much as an example of how ballsy George was but of how he had a true sense of fairness. It was not until I was middle-aged that I realized the absurdity of this, crusading for the right to pay protection money only once.

Another tale that set the moral bar low involved my father's cousin Jake. Of the generation between George and my father, Jake represented America to my dad, who loved and relied upon him until his untimely death in early middle age. Jake started off in the business as a kid, running errands, odd jobs. He had worked his way up to the showroom when a buyer proposed taking a large lot, if Jake would throw in the girl—the coat model—as a tip. Jake was streetwise in his own way, but this stunned him. What to do? He excused himself, and rushed to see George. George told him what to say to the buyer, and had Jake memorize it. "This is not a whorehouse and I am not a pimp." Jake ran back, happy to declare it.

I'd always loved the story—the feisty kid, the corrupt buyer, the young lady wrapped in a stylish coat, my grandfather's God-like pronouncement. But here again, we were proud to not be pimps, to not be running a whorehouse, just as we'd been proud to not be out and out gangsters. This seemed like very low standards.

My grandfather's gangsterism extended to his philanthropy, which was itself vast and generous, yet self-serving. As a small child, I too had been encouraged to be philanthropic. I had saved up part of my allowance week after week to join the Bronx Zoo. I would be a member, with free admission, discounts, and best of all, a members' garden party with a private viewing of a rare platypus. I was about ten years old, and ready to give my money to the zoo, when Grandpa George got wind of my stash.

We were alone, on the wraparound screened porch of my parents' house. He loomed over me, and demanded I hand over my savings to donate to plant trees in Israel. But my goal was already set. Israel, no. Platypus, yes. George yelled and screamed, towering over me. My father appeared like a deus ex machina, also shouting, "Leave her alone! It's her money!"

I went to the members' party and ate finger sandwiches and chocolate cookies shaped like leaves. I saw the remarkable platypus. I was the only child there, the only young person who had bought herself a membership. Old ladies in hats smiled at me. I planted not one twig in Israel.

My Father's Atheism

My father did not believe in God, but he was not without belief. His atheism was a kind of religion, and he brought full fervor to it. My father's articles of faith were that there was no God, particularly not the God of the Jews. Anyone who believed in God was worse than wrong—a believer was a child. Scorn dripped from my father's lips when he said the word "child." It seemed to me, child that I was, that being a child was just as bad as believing in God.

Since God was never described or investigated, we just took it on faith that God was not for us. But since I had no idea what God was, I was not completely spiritually crippled. I had a strong love of nature combined with a firm sense of ethics—both from my father. I also had mystical experiences of oneness and connection that I simply found pleasurable when I was young. These things were just part of my inner world, like being able to make things happen in my dreams or ALMOST seeing the wings of flower fairies. I had nightly hypnogogic experiences of glittering colored lights and dots before I fell sleep. Sometimes I saw beautiful dancers in pink tutus. My friend Laurel and I lay on a hillside and fell asleep, promising to appear in each other's dreams. We did. I took this all in stride—it was a natural part of my world to know and accept that there were realms other than the ordinary one.

My father also hated what he called "mysticism." In retrospect, I think he was using the word correctly; he hated the experience in which a person felt at one with something larger. It is obvious that my father himself was given to spontaneous bouts of connection, particularly inspired by art and music. He once confessed to me, when he was quite old, that when he was alone he'd dance naked in celebration to Beethoven and Mozart. He once ran out of the Uffizi Gallery in Florence, dazzled and overwhelmed by the painting. "Those paintings were going to grab my soul," he confided, sitting panting on the museum steps.

His character was surely at odds with his beliefs. He forbade us from going to synagogue and from prayer, even of the private sort. I once came upon my little sister praying and was as shocked and terrified as if I'd found her torturing a kitten. This was forbidden territory.

I did go to synagogue for the bat-mitzvahs of friends, and the slightly pathetic attempts at "boy-girl" parties that ensued. I was "allowed" to attend church with a friend because she was black, and her church a bastion of civil rights activity. Although this church was quite alien to me culturally—it had a gospel choir, fiery preaching, and church lady hats—I felt instantly relaxed there. This feeling continued for me as I eventually went to synagogue, studied with Hassids, married a Zen monk, and worshipped with friends in disparate settings from Catholic monasteries to Christian Science services to Quaker meetings.

It turned out I liked religion. I studied Hebrew and koans and prayer. When it comes to check the box, I say I believe in God. Actually, there is little about belief here. I experience God. If I did not, I would not care.

I also experienced my father. In a world without God, he, my father, reigned supreme. This was, shockingly for the feminist thinker he professed to be, a kind of absolute patriarchy. But fortunately I also did not believe completely in my father.

Grand Jury

My father's favorite movie was *The Godfather*. He identified with the college-educated son who'd served in World War Two but who was nonetheless somehow forced into his father's corrupt business.

My mother hated it when we talked like that. "They weren't gangsters," she'd say. "Don't romanticize the garment industry." It is odd now to think that she considered gangsterism romantic. Frankly, I found it frightening. It was scary because the men in my family were not as they appeared. They seemed to live by varying codes, and have the ability to plunge into brutality. As a child, this was apparent to me on a visceral level. As an adult, when I read Isaac Babel's stories of red-headed Jewish smugglers and killers in the port of Odessa, I recognized the type. The Sagan men were not of the yeshiva and the shtetl, pale and victimized. They were the opposite.

My father was called before a Grand Jury that was convened in Manhattan to investigate the garment industry about a decade after he had left the business. The investigation was into the corrupt practices of the industry, but focused mainly on federal tax evasion, a hallmark of a business run on kickbacks, bribes, and cash.

Manhattan's crusading and ambitious district attorney led the charge. He was going after crime that had been allowed to flourish undisturbed. My father, who was about fifty years old then, was supposed to testify in the fall. He spent the summer pacing about the family's pleasant beach house muttering the words "statute of limitations" under his breath. "They want to know where the bodies are buried," he'd joke, but grimly.

"1952," he'd say abruptly, kicking an ottoman. "How long ago was that?" He'd count backwards. "What's the statute of limitations on..." Then he'd shut up abruptly, as if stopped by memory.

My sisters were teenagers that summer, and boy crazy. My father, paying even less attention to other people than usual, lent one of them the car and mentioned no curfew.

My father went to bed. At three o'clock in the morning the phone rang.

It was the District Attorney. If it had been the SS my father's blood pressure and heart rate could not have sky-rocketed more quickly.

Sweating, he could barely grunt into the receiver.

"Mr. Sagan," the voice said, "where is my son? He is out with your daughter."

My father gasped for air, hilarious with relief. "They went to the beach," he said, not noticing how bad that sounded to the father of a teenager in the middle of the night.

"If you see him, tell him to come home."

Soon enough, headlights pierced the foggy driveway. My sister, no doubt sandy, emerged, having dropped the boy off at his house. My father paid little attention to this escapade. He was euphoric—his crusading nemesis had called but not to drag him off at dawn to be shot. He felt saved.

But he still had to testify. That autumn, his own attorney instructed him to say as little as possible, to answer questions minimally, to not volunteer information.

"Mr. Sagan," the DA enquired. "The garment industry is notoriously corrupt. And you were a leader in its business for many years…"

"I've heard it is very corrupt," agreed my father. Or at least that was all of the exchange he ever reported to us.

Florence, Italy

My father, in his prime, was not a calm person. He could be adventurous, but would suddenly panic, as he did on the night train to Florence, Italy.

We were abroad, the six of us, each with a large brown canvas suitcase. The train stopped at the Florence train station—Firenze—for three minutes. Then it went north, no doubt into the Balkans or Bulgaria, carrying those other passengers—gypsies, guitarists, soldiers, assassins—behind the iron curtain.

So we were instructed to hurl first our heavy suitcases and then ourselves on to the platform. Before the train even stopped, my father was cramming his suitcase through a cracked window and, heedless of four children who might be left behind, he leapt from the train.

He was hysterical, but unscathed. We survived our disembarkation and saw Madonnas draped in blue, and Jesus bleeding on numerous crosses, odd fare for Jews. We ate pasta.

blue mussel shells open—
the briny taste
I will acquire

I often think I would have been happier if I'd stayed on the train, vanished into Macedonia or Armenia, been in my thirties when the Berlin Wall came down and gone some place like Norway to work in the hotel business.

fountain's sprawling gods,
cathedral's great shut doors,
my father points, points.

Part 3

Gone

I was in the Dallas airport. Not unusual. For three decades I'd visited my parents, progressively older and sicker, changing in Dallas.

I bought a paperback and a candy bar at one of the little newsstand concessions. The cashier was a dazzling, tall blonde, maybe in her thirties, with cold, blue eyes. But her accent wasn't Scandinavian, I couldn't place it.

"So where are you from?" I asked. This question has often led me into interesting conversations with strangers. But this conversation wasn't going in that direction.

She looked blank, horrified, grief-stricken. "You won't have heard of it," she said.

"Try me."

"It isn't there any more," she said. "It's gone."

And then repeated, "It's gone."

Between that first and second statement, I got something. "It" wasn't just gone. "They" were gone too. People. Family. Friends. Neighbors. Gone.

She turned away. I went to my gate.

Over the years, I've wondered where this place was. The Balkans, I've concluded. Some part of Bosnia. Or the idea of a nation like Yugoslavia. She sounded a little bit Eastern European. What's gone? I look at the map.

What's gone—the borderlands of my grandparents in the Ukraine, the Jewish lower east side, a parochial New Jersey, my childhood, the person I was before I got sick, the person I would have been if I'd stayed on the east coast, my first husband who died young...no, this isn't what I mean. It's not gone because I can remember, and what I don't remember I invent and believe to be true.

So much of what I'm writing these days poses questions of tense, of the syntax that creates meaning. What subject matter is truly mine? Does what I observed— perhaps innocently, no doubt partially—about other people count? What about the violence and corruption in those close to me that I've tried to distance myself from? The easy answer is to say—yes, it is all mine. But I'm not ready to rest there.

Where do I place my mind, my intention, my imagination.

What happened to the blond woman at the newsstand was history. And I on the outside, asking the unanswerable.

Things That Ought To Stay Put

But Don't

the number of planets in the solar system
gender
the past
my parents' minds
shoes, keys, glasses
God
a genetic predisposition
the San Andreas fault
my faults
yours, too
sea level
measurements
currency
the border
being asleep
being awake
the food pyramid
properties of light

The Beginning of The End

At the age of eighty-four, my father cracked up his car on the Bourne Bridge, a WPA engineering feat that spans the Cape Cod Canal. He was driving a Toyota Prius, my mother a Subaru wagon. They were making their annual trek from New Jersey to the Wood's Hole ferry, which would transport them across the sound to the Island of Martha's Vineyard to their beach house in the town of Chilmark. This journey had assumed mythic proportions and was fraught with terror—the terror of missing the ferry, which had never happened.

My father had appeared disoriented earlier in the trip. They'd broken the drive and slept in a motel. My mother had vaguely and hesitantly attempted to keep my father from driving. But he insisted. No doubt screamed and yelled, possibly slapped or punched. And so he drove. Cracking the car against one of the support pillars of the bridge itself. Ambulance. Sirens. The hospital in Falmouth. Not a stroke, they said. Low sodium. He appeared drunk, or deranged, and temporarily lost his license.

Why did my mother allow him to drive? This is a simple rational sentence. Does one allow a charging lion or a hurricane? My father's tantrums were notorious.

I was in Iceland when I heard this news. My friend Kathleen and I had an apartment on a lake, and a looming view of the enormous volcano Mt. Hekla. Steam rose from the lake. It was light all night. Kath and I were very happy. We had come to write and sightsee and had left our husbands at home. They, despite their protested adoration of us, declined our invitation to expensive faraway Iceland.

We didn't have working cell phones. I went to the convenience store and bought a phone card for about fifty dollars. The store was charming. It had the usual convenience foods, a bit of produce, a lot of salted fish, yarn, expensive hand knit sweaters, and an adorable staff of three teenagers.

There was a handsome guy and two slightly younger girls. All good-looking in that Icelandic way of appearing as Irish as Viking. The girls flirted continuously with the boy, who was ostensibly their supervisor. They ruffled his hair, tossed things out of reach, giggled by the hour.

I took the phone card to the nearby Edda Hotel. It was a long sprawl of Scandinavian modern that was still quiet in early summer. I found the pay phone in the basement.

"Don't come," said my mother. Right then, of course, I had no intention of rushing back. My father had been hospitalized briefly, taken off his usual diuretic, and discharged. The Prius had been towed and fixed. My sister and brother-in-law transported both cars and parents and deposited them at the beach house. There, my father took to his bed for the summer, complaining of a pain in his leg.

"It's shock," he told me. "It's the shock. I lost my license."

"But dad," I said, dangling the phone cord in the basement, "do you feel like yourself?" He sounded so strange.

"My leg," he said. "My leg. It hurts. My leg."

I never had a normal conversation with my father again.

But what was the last normal conversation I'd had with him?

My father was an eccentric misanthrope, something I did not truly realize until I was in my forties. It is possible I never had what could be considered a normal conversation with him, ever. He liked to talk about intellectual subjects—political, psychoanalytic, anthropological. This was his mode to me from the age when I could first—haltingly—follow.

My father retired from the garment business when he was about forty. He then became, although it seems incredible and unlikely, an autodidactic sociologist whose gods were Marx and Freud.

It was an odd way to be raised. My father would quiz my friends who'd come to dinner about his most recent preoccupation, cannibalism.

"Would you rather eat someone you know or someone you don't?" he'd ask, and then move on to menstrual huts.

I found him embarrassing, of course. However, my mother worshipped him, and he seemed to highly value himself. He was different from other fathers, and in my family that meant better.

I had seen my father just a few weeks before he cracked up over the Cape Cod Canal. We'd talked about Hamlet, and the plots of operas. He had driven me and my husband Rich to catch a train at Newark. His driving was terrifying. He veered wildly. Cut people off. Yelled. I made a private vow to never be his passenger again. Subsequent events made that easy to keep.

"Don't come," said my mother. Her voice travelled to Iceland, and later to Santa Fe, when I was back home in New Mexico. "It would be absurd for you to come. Why would you come?"

"To help?" I suggested.

"That would be absurd," she said.

I called every few days. Then the fall semester started, and I returned to work.

That is when my mother said, "Come immediately. I can't stand it any more." She sobbed, a regular occurrence.

The best I could manage was Rosh Hashana, a few weeks later. They were back in New Jersey. We tried a few of our usual routines, which didn't work very well.

We headed out for the Metropolitan Museum of Art. My father, snappish, disoriented, and even cruel, reduced my mother to tears in the cab. At the museum, he rushed in and attempted to obtain entrance tickets at the coat check. My mother continued to weep. I eventually abandoned them on a bench, saying I'd meet them in an hour.

I went straight to the hall with the giant wall mural of the Buddha, and the enormous Chinese terra cotta Bodhisattvas. As a teenager, I'd loved the peace of these rooms. I could feel the Buddhas humming as I sat for a long time.

My parents managed to sell the house and move to Boston to be near one of my sisters. My father would have a major stroke and become aphasic, although regaining the ability to walk and to speak a little. He would continue to complain about his leg, although no scan revealed anything and no PT created relief.

"I think it started," I told my sister, "when dad drove off the Bourne Bridge."

"Mir," she chided me. "He didn't go off. He just hit a siding."

In my imagination, the car crashes through the guard rail and plunges to the bottom of the canal. Frogmen dive to rescue my father. I tell them to leave him where he is.

What We Shared

waiting for the dark water to rise
as it does every night, uncontrolled
in dream, rises
over the prow
of the boat where we sit
I ask if you see the great beast
swimming through the muck
you say you know it is there
waiting for the breech as if for birth
from water into air
waiting for the hidden to become visible
and knowing that it never will.

Wrack Line

Noman's is an island
Off an island off a cape off the mainland
Left to gulls and
Army bombers' target practice.

A cairn of stone
Might mark the dead
A pile to mark
A boundary
(land/sea
here/gone)
A cache of memory.

Wind and waves have cut
A forgery into rock
These runes don't spell a charm
Or mark arrival
Or departure from these shores
Mean anything at all...

Sandpipers scurry
Out of their own calligraphy
Like Chinese hermits writing on a stone
And wave erases
What you cannot own
Or even transliterate.

Things come and go
Not Vikings, lured here as we'd hoped
By summer (as were we)
But passage of a cloud or thought.
The man who carried me on his back
Is old, and bent
As if
Looking for something
In the sand.

House with blue shutters sits on the bluff,
Pale Indian pipes that might
Be seen to glow
Inside a paperweight...
Human life isn't
As easy
As crossing a field
And crossing this field
Isn't that easy.

Historians say
It never was,
This wasn't Vinland
Despite its grapes and vines

Despite our desire
That this island remain
In time
And be admired
Be longed for by those dragon ships
That wanted everywhere else
London, Paris, the Volga
So why not us?

My father tells me of a cave
Where painted beasts roam undisturbed
Here arrow finds what it must seek
At the beginning of the world.
First quarry, and the urge to dominate
Not just hunger
That drives this hunter to praise
What he will catch and eat.

In a darkness
As Neolithic
As it is familiar
Behind closed eyes
I see them still
Out by the horizon's sill.
Whale's way, swan's way, a riddle given
The answer
Now
Must lie within.

Noman's lies in the haze
Just the nesting terns disturbed

Or wars
That seethe
Half a world away
To us it disrupts
A summer's day
We lie sunbathing on the strand.

End

My father had a massive stroke, and became aphasic. After this, he lived for more than two years. He regained his ability to walk, and to speak a bit. But he was a frail husk. A cool spring breeze was too much for him, and he whimpered in sunlight, preferring instead to walk in the underground parking garage beneath my parents' apartment.

The next full-blown crisis, the penultimate one, came about two years later, at Thanksgiving. I was already someplace unusual when it happened. I was sitting at a desk at Thoreau Farm, the homestead where Henry David was born. I had two days there, communing with the Transcendentalist philosopher. I had bought the opportunity to write there at the Thoreau Society's auction. It was difficult to get there, as I was a nervous urban driver with a terror of Boston's notorious loop highway, Route 128. I printed out Google directions, but became worried when Lexington Street turned into Moody and then to Common. I got lost at Hanscom Air Force Base and felt humiliated when the person I asked for directions glared at me. I then overshot, and eventually asked the turbaned owner of a convenience store for help and went back, left on Old Bedford Road, and right on Virginia.

The green lichen showed bright on the oak trees that had shed piles of brown leaves. The desk was green, the floor painted an authentic nineteenth century color: mustard. I was eating a peanut butter sandwich and writing haiku by hand when my sister called.

owl calls
the one you never see-
winter pond

oak leaves
at the window panes—
scattered thoughts

paper wasps gone,
empty twig nest, I'm also
not at home

Concord's wet sky
full of winter birds—
I read Shiki

is the "I"
really the poet—
small white breasted bird

half a dream
unraveling like a ball
of dark blue yarn

past Dunkin' Donuts
and the air force base—
Thoreau's birthplace

the philosopher
walks the railroad track—
swallows at dusk.

My father was in the hospital again. This time I had only to brave Route 128 and Boston drivers to arrive. I was so frazzled I did not attempt my overland route, and to my surprise got back in half the time.

fine scissors snipped
silhouette of those now dead
in black paper;
nothing in the world
but the ticking of the clock.

Electra

This was the only incident in which I was on the scene in a timely fashion. My father, still aphasic from the first stroke and now incapacitated by multiple small ones, lay in the bed surrounded by beeping machines. Sensitive as always, he would shriek and yell if touched or if a tech inserted a needle or tore off a sticky pastie. He did smile, eat some pastry I brought, and say a few odd things. Then he whipped down the sheet, pointed to his crotch, and said in a perfectly full sentence: "What am I supposed to do about this?"

There was a tech in the room, and I, absurdly mindful of the hyper-modest man my father had once been said, "Dad, maybe you'd like to cover up."

Again, perfectly, he retorted, "Maybe I wouldn't like to cover up."

We figured out that he needed to pee, but that was not the import in my mind. In a way my father was asking some basic questions. What was he supposed to do about being a man? And in the most basic sense—

showing me his organ of procreation—what was he supposed to do about being my father?

A few weeks later, my dad went into hospice. He refused to eat, drink, or take any medication. I was in Arizona. I tried to feel my father, process him, without the hullabaloo of white noise of being around my family in my head. After all, my father loved Arizona, and had introduced me to it. I was eleven years old during a cross-country train trip. I heard my father's voice in my head, twice. I was in Bisbee, debating the cost of two ultra-groovy, tie-dyed sets of leggings. "Get both," I heard him say, "who knows when you'll pass this way again." I did.

The second time, in a funky roadside cafe I heard him urge, "Don't get the pasta, they might ruin it. In this part of the world, steak is a safe bet." I ordered it medium rare and it was delicious.

We spent a night in derelict lodging on the less accessible side of the Chiricahuas. The view of barren, jagged mountains was spectacular, the bathroom stained and peeling. Here, I made a list of everything I hated about my father and then one of everything I loved. Surprisingly, the two lists were the same length.

We drove home through the bootheel of New Mexico, land so remote it seemed not to border on a real country like Mexico but on some loneliness that could not be contained in specific time and place.

I unpacked my suitcase and soon packed again, taking a black dress. I landed in Logan Airport late at night, and checked in to an airport hotel. This had become my routine many times a year when preparing to visit my parents. I ate a lobster roll from room service and went to sleep. My father died, a few minutes past midnight, a half hour away in the cold suburban dark.

A hundred days after my father died, I saw him in a vision before actual sleep. He was hiking in a lovely forested landscape with a big lake. It looked like northern Vermont. He was wearing his antiquated hiking boots, which he'd bought for his honeymoon and worn when we went down the Grand Canyon. He looked middle-aged, and cheerful. "Hi," he said. "I'm going off to see Robert, want to come along?" As Robert was my long dead first husband, I just said, "No thanks." "Well," my dad said, without any show of disappointment in the lack of my company, "I expect to see your mother soon."

And he walked on without me.

It's Snowing

It's snowing in my father's brain
time to say good-bye
to understanding brush and comb
he says: I have escaped from hell

gray matter like November rain
turns sleet to hail to crystalline
he knows who is the president
but not if the sea is dry or wet

thought falls like flakes, six-sided, slick
even moonlight or honeycomb might melt
thinking of you, or not, with love's regret
I've finished what I started to say
even without a strict refrain
it's snowing in my father's brain.

St. Death

Santa Muerte is not enclosed
behind the grill
of a roadside shrine on the border

but like a descanso
might be
anywhere, everywhere, a corner

even in the automatic
thumbed cross
of gangsters' mouths

or those who die
with chapped prayers on their lips
or those who curse

saying: fuck this
or those tethered
to the morphine drip

a cavalero
printed on a scarf, socks
a sugar cookie

I think of you—
and you—and you
the increasing crew

of my beloved
half-remembered dead
and lean on my cane

on the snowy path
in the Chiricahuas
and think about nothing but

lichen on rock
and time's lovely
gnarled driftwood.

Representation

bonsai represents "tree"
but also is itself a tree
bent in the direction the wind, even if
imaginary, is blowing

scholar's stone on the desk
shapes a terrain of cracks and slopes,
liftable mountain

the man who was my father
sits with his damaged hands
in his lap, searching
for a word
but still might make
a small joke
sarcastic and affectionate

although I don't
sentimentally
remember what
he showed me
stars? fireflies?

and yet
it must have been
this world.

Ties That Bind

When I was a teenager, I'd hide in my father's cedar closet and try on his ties—around my waist as a sash, around my forehead as a hippie headband.

I was sixty years old when he died. I took three of his ties, cut them up, and knitted them along with wire, yarn, lace, string, and scraps into mourning pieces.

His ties were narrow. When they went out of fashion he held on to them, waiting for the style to come back in. And it did, although by then he no longer wore ties or anything formal.

He was many people, more than I am.

Hollyhocks

My father hated hollyhocks. How can you hate a flower. He never said why, but he did. As children, we'd torment him on a walk or drive, exclaiming Look! Hollyhocks! And then we'd say how pretty they were, how colorful. I love them, but interestingly they are the only local flower not growing in my garden. The neighborhood is full of them, not much the worse for recent hail.

black hollyhocks,
every summer
I lose
all ambition,
and wait for rain

To Orpheus

I'm glad to live in a world that includes morphine.

This isn't the time
for sentiment
or to praise
pears and apples.

Love was my dripline until I awakened
and my hair was gray.

I'll want
the death
that has my name
on it.

Don't protest too much or say you are
coming with me.

I know
we're going to the same place
whether together
or alone.

Acid, 1971

The click click click of the legal tap on the phone in my father's house confronted us every time we picked up the receiver. It drove my friends—a bunch of small time drug dealers—crazy, although it was not aimed at them. It was aimed at my father, because this was the height of the war in Viet Nam and the president of a peace organization of which my father was treasurer had gone to visit Hanoi. Click, click, click. My father was a happy man. The most powerful government in the world was concerned with him. He was arrested, Mirandized, released over a matter of cash at a rally. His name appeared on Nixon's enemies list. He was audited on his taxes straight through until the first year of Carter's administration.

Click, click. What the fuck is that? asked Joey Patmos. He was my friend my junior year in high school, skinny, dirty blond, wrapped in an old army jacket, Greek, from two towns over. Joey announced that he was coming over and I tried to dissuade him. It was dinnertime, and he sounded high. I wasn't much of a druggie myself. The sight of a close friend's little brother hurling himself through a plate glass window tripping at a party had been enough to reinforce my natural caution. But I could talk you down.

My mother, despite the disintegration of civilization around her, still believed in dinner. She was terrified, though, that our father's activities would lead to the kidnapping of one of my younger siblings. "Look," she said desperately to my father, pointing to an article in the *New York Times* in which he was described as a millionaire opposed to the war. "They say millionaire—you know what that means. Some lunatic will go and kidnap the kids for money." The Lindbergh baby was as clear in my mother's imagination as if it were yesterday. My father paid no attention. I'd barely tucked into a nice chicken breast with rice and broccoli when Joey arrived and I hustled him upstairs to my room. He was in a very bad part of his trip— the non-blissy paranoid part—that appeared also to be just the start. He slumped down at the foot of my four-poster bed, rapidly opening and closing his eyes. It had been raining, and his hair was matted. I kept him stashed in the bedroom while doing homework, fighting with my sister, even, eventually, brushing my teeth. Every so often Joey said, "I'm going to die," and I said, "no you're not." It was a school night and I had to get rid of him. Click, click, click. I called a friend of ours who lived around the block, hustled Joey Patmos out into the rain. I watched him walk away. I was as alone in the world as if I were on an ice floe.

Time passes. Thirty-four years later I am sitting in my backyard on a summer's day with my father. My daughter is a teenager, and she has been drifting in and out all weekend with her friends. A tall boy on a bicycle comes over. He is introduced, shakes my father's hand, and disappears into my daughter's room. My father looks pained, perhaps, I think, by the boy behind closed doors.

"Remember when you were that age?" says my father.

"Yes," I say, which is quite true

"And they arrested me that time and read me my Miranda rights?" He looks happy all over again.

"Mom was scared," I say.

"Nothing was going to happen," he says. "It wasn't like McCarthyism."

I nod.

"That time that Joey Patmos came over," he says, "that evening...."

I am completely startled. "You remember that?"

"He was on LSD, wasn't he?" says my father. "Some kind of drugs?"

"Yes, LSD, he certainly was."

"I'm sorry," says my father. "I wanted to help you but I had no idea how. So I just didn't say anything."

I listen for the click that is sometimes in my brain, but it is silent.

Letter To My Younger Self

Dear Mir,

Just want to say to you, my younger self, that contrary to all your beliefs, you are totally fine. I know you hate yourself and are convinced you will never get out of New Jersey. Let me just say you will see the northern lights over Greenland, San Francisco from the back of a motorcycle, and millions of acres of salt flats beneath the moon.

I know you feel stifled. You want to know about death, and you can relax—you'll find out a lot about it, maybe more than you bargained for. Do not worry, you will not spend the rest of your life lying on the mildewed couch on your mother's front porch reading D.H. Lawrence.

You will find more fascinating things to read. You will know monks and poets and junkies. You will have a child, a foster daughter, seven nieces and nephews, and two husbands. You will be in the audience for a play at the state penitentiary, performed by inmates. There will be drink, drugs, waking dreams, hallucinations, koans, and long dull afternoons.

Terrible things will happen to you—violence, bereavement, fear for others—and you will not enjoy these things but you will not be bored. Women's clothes are also going to get much better—lots of flowy, ethnic items and big dangling earrings that can be worn to work. You won't have to wear heels. Women will stop wearing girdles. There are going to be streaming movies and email and blogs instead of mimeo machines. Men will love you—not all men everywhere but just enough for a lifetime of entertainment.

Oh please cheer up, sad and dumb younger self. Do not fall off a roof or overdose or die of swine flu. A lot of things are going to happen to you and you will be comfortably dressed and not in New Jersey.

Love,

The Older You

Living in the Triassic

I walked crosstown in the rain
To the Museum of Natural History
In search of what I'd seen in the desert
The polychrome Chinle layer, which here
Lies under Newark, New Jersey.
The past can't help but break through
In outcroppings, chock full
Of fossils, small intent dinosaurs,
And their preserved footprints, a placental
Cache of eggs.

This was not
The Petrified Forest
Where the great mineralized trunks
Of former trees
Calved out of the earth itself
But rather the personal past

A museum full of displaced objects:
    a jar of buttons
    a suitcase full of leaves
    onion rings
    the hidden violets of childhood
    the Temple of Jerusalem in a bottle

All these maps are the maps of time.
Is memory fixed, like trauma,
Or can it shift?
Gone forever
The chestnut tree
My grandfather planted,
The red Chinese mirror
With its silvered backing
Disintegrating
To an unreadable calligraphy.

But you can imagine
What it says...
The little replica
Of the Parthenon
Shatters
In my suitcase,
Trying to preserve
What cannot be preserved
Confusing souvenir
With memory.
Across Broadway
Strobe lights lit the dance studio
Until the photographer
Posed
One draped figure
In the corner
And snapped the frame.

I saw the dustless mirror
Reflect Newark, New Jersey
I did not dust it
But it was perfectly clear
Reflecting cattails, barbed wire, prison, airport.
In all versions, my childhood disappears
The developer cuts down
The copper beeches
I still fly over in my dreams.

New Jersey

"Why are you calling?" my father asks.

It is the afternoon of September 11th. My father lives twelve minutes from New York City if there is no traffic. I have spent hours dialing and re-dialing his number and finally—miraculously—the circuits don't overload and put me through.

"Why are you calling?" he asks.

"Because..." I stumble in surprise. "You know, the bombing, the towers are down..."

"I'm in New Jersey," my father says. "That is Manhattan. I'm in New Jersey."

I also was once in New Jersey, was raised there, a place of vendetta, sexual warfare, and imminent disaster. I have been waiting for something to happen to New Jersey ever since I was a child, since the Cuban Missile Crisis.

When I was sixteen years old, I thought that apocalypse had arrived. I was lying in bed as I was wont to do, feet on my pillow, head by the foot end. My window faced south. And there I saw a pink mushroom cloud on the horizon swell to its perfect shape.

I rushed across the hall to my parent's bedroom, disturbing them. "I saw a mushroom cloud!" I shouted.

"You always exaggerate," my mother said. Then the shock waves hit the house, breaking two windows. It was not the Russians but a refinery blowing sky high in an industrial town near Elizabeth. No one was killed but this was not a place that anyone went to sleep at night.

I have always exaggerated. Once, in a nice family style fish restaurant I sat facing the water when I saw fireworks explode over the marina.

"Look!" I told everybody. "Look! Turn around. Fireworks!"

No one turned to look. No one believed me. No one cared what I saw. I must be exaggerating.

Eventually, my first husband, the only person at the table who had not known me as a child, turned. It was Bastille Day, and he saw golden flowers unfolding—both reflected in and dissolving over the water.

Island In The Sky

Rim sandstone
Once an ancient shore

Now redrock cliffs
Calve colossi, pharaohs
Temples, colonnades

To imagine the sea here
Is to dream

Great swaths of desert varnish
Eon's paintbrush,
An arch frames vastness

Air, ledge, fall, desert
On and on

Fossil layer preserves
Ripple marks
Impression of raindrops

To hear the sea
Is to know you are asleep

Aperture
Lacuna
Sky blue hole

Where rock shale was tide flats
And salt cracks your lips.

And to rub the sand
From your eyelids
Is to awake

IN BLUEBEARD'S CASTLE is set in Avenir, a twentieth century,
geometric type designed by
Adrian Frutiger